LAUGHING BUDDHA
WEEPING SUFI

LAUGHING BUDDHA
WEEPING SUFI

poems

NOVEMBER 7, 2003 – JANUARY 10, 2004

Daniel Abdal-Hayy Moore

THE ECSTATIC EXCHANGE

2005

Philadelphia

For quotes any longer than those for critical articles and reviews,
contact:
The Ecstatic Exchange,
6470 Morris Park Road, Philadelphia, PA 19151-2403
email: abdalhayy@danielmoorepoetry.com

First Edition
Published by *The Ecstatic Exchange,*
6470 Morris Park Road, Philadelphia, PA 19151-2403

Designed by Abdallateef Whiteman

Cover design Abdallateef Whiteman
Cover collage by the author
Back cover photograph by Malika Moore

Dedicated to the teachers:

Gene Gonder, first genius,
Marco Antonio Montes de Oca, first poet,
Sensei Shunryu Suzuki, Zen Master,
Shaykh Sayyidi Muhammad ibn al-Habib
(*may God be pleased with him*)
—and the living continuation of his teachings—
Shaykh Muhammad Rahim Bawa Muhaiyaddeen,
(*may God be pleased with him*)
Faruk Dilaver, sweet sohbets from the akhira,
Baji Tayyaba Khanum, deepest devotion,

the earth is not bereft
of Light

CONTENTS

AUTHOR'S INTRODUCTION

SOMEONE ASKED A ZEN MASTER, "*What is Buddha nature?*" and the master put his shoes on his head. Mulla Nasruddin lost his keys one night, and was looking for them under a street lamp. Someone asked him why he was looking for them there, since he'd said he lost them somewhere else. "*Because here at least there's some light to see by!*"

Do we live in an Age of Reason, or an age like most others, filled with both reason and unreason, joy and tragedy, teaching of The Way (never mind for now which one) and resistance to the teaching? Human nature is a constant battlefield of dichotomies and reconciliations.

I first tasted real spiritual centering with Sensei Shunryu Suzuki, a great saintly Zen Master, in San Francisco in the early 1960s. He was a model of enlightenment. Always maintaining spiritual poise, light and easily inspired to a gentle laughter by whatever foible or sweetness was available to the world or his mind, but also deep and profound in his compassionate earnestness for our welfare and for the full "accomplishment" of our Zen practice. Muslims occasionally express a reluctance about Buddhists because of their often professed disbelief in a single Divine God. But in one talk Suzuki gave he said that Buddhists don't *disbelieve* in God, they simply don't talk about it. Yet I always found their sutras and treatises to be filled with that exalted dimension I might now call "God-consciousness." And the proof positive of their spirituality, really, was in the radiance of their actions and in their caring for each other and the minute details of life with a real reverence that can only come from true spiritual teaching. Their "theism" is reflected more in their equanimity and openness, and their sense of a flexible immediacy to whatever the universe confronts them with.

Then when I became a Muslim in 1969 in Berkeley, California, I simultaneously entered a Sufi Tariqa whose Master, Sayyedina Shaykh Muhammd ibn al-Habib, lived in Meknes, Morocco. When I sat in his presence, may Allah be pleased with him, I was in the shadow of a giant mountain of light, an overflowing of that God-consciousness, a manifestation of Allah's Mercy, Compassion and Knowledge in human form, whose very proximity brought both tranquility and a sudden soul's awakening, a deeper alertness. And his disciples were people who had been with him most of their lives, for he was over 100 years old, and some of them were grandchildren of his first disciples, and they also partook of that sweetness and that delicacy of being that is also stronger than the trunks of redwood trees and more resilient than any flood of social or personal tragedy. These people saw Allah's manifestation in everything, which in its way is not that distant from seeing the Buddha-nature in everything. Each is a way of being truly human in a transparent world of signs and meanings. But Allah is the Judge.

Then there are those who actually compare the ways of Taoist and Zen mystics and poets with those of Sufism, and recently the American shaykh, Hamza Yusuf, has written, "Both the Maliki and Hanafi schools have traditionally accepted *jizya* and *dhimmi* status from Hindus and Buddhists, as both religions possess Books as the foundation of their religions and retain cosmologies so sophisticated as to instill respect and study in the west..." * A recent title from Harvard University is, *The Dao of Muhammad: A Cultural History of Muslims in Late Imperial China*.

When these poems began insisting themselves in my frequent night vigils, I was struck by something a teacher of ours once said, that for the Buddhist enlightenment is a mental awakening, whose experience is that of a state of delighted or liberating laughter, a Satori flash of spacious detachment. While for a Sufi, enlightenment is more a bursting of the heart, *fana*, a total effacement in Allah, whose expression is more often tears, of ecstasy as well as, later, of grief over separation from that epiphany and a recognition of one's momentous shortcomings before God. This is not to say that the Buddhist enlightenment is not of the heart, nor that of the Sufi not also of the intellect. But generally speaking, the Buddhist laughs, the Sufi weeps: for both, that is the apex moment of the world.

Am I advocating a similarity of Paths between Buddhism and Islam? I've been a Muslim now for thirty-five years, and for me God's statement in the Qur'an that Islam (or "submission to Divine Reality") is the final revelation to mankind has made universal sense, in spite of modern betrayals by misguided Muslims. But we must have mutual respect and honor every worthy Path, and be supportive of any true and noble Way that leads people to stronger, sweeter, more peaceful and enlightened lives.

* *Seasons*, Spring-Summer, 2005

So Laughing Buddha and Weeping Sufi, the two protagonists of these poems set in a certain shifting and watery landscape of remembrance and imaginal realities, are not that dissimilar to the characters in *Waiting for Godot* by Samuel Beckett, except that they're not waiting. They're *there*. And they're not strictly a dichotomy, but perhaps two sides of a single soul. It is said of the Prophet Muhammad, peace be upon him, that he was the most laughing of men. And the Buddha? Somber and sober, laconic in his teaching to the point of silence.

A Sufi friend wrote to me recently of a trip he made to the desert of Morocco to visit a true living saint: "I was struck by how, as he poured forth prayers and blessings to us individually and collectively, the things he said were said in a voice that made me think at first he was weeping until I saw that it was actually laughter but sounded like weeping. And I remember thinking at the time that perhaps this was it, this was the fruit of the way reduced to its essence: this endless outpouring of prayers and blessings and thanks and remembrance flowing forth on a wave of laughter and tears."

And that same friend alerted me to a verse (*ayat*: sign) from the Qur'an (53:42) that seems to sum it up best:

That it is He who brings about both laughter and tears

I pray that the various activities and "conversations" of *Laughing Buddha and Weeping Sufi* will bring the taste of this particular landscape to the reader as well.

Note: when I went to give these poems titles (I had been numbering them in their notebook) I was inspired to dash out a title without looking at the poem first, so the titles are actually independent of the poems, "chance" titles" as sit were, slightly goofy Haikus that are either in harmony or at odds with their subsequent poem.

LAUGHING BUDDHA WEEPING SUFI

That it is He who brings about both laughter and tears

Excess of sorrow laughs. Excess of joy weeps.

~ WILLIAM BLAKE

"Inayat Khan smiled at me and asked, '*Mr. Senzaki,*
will you tell me what the significance of Zen is?'
I remained silent for a little while, and then smiled at him.
He smiled back at me. Our dialogue was over."

1 AN ORANGE SUNSET SITS ON A BLUE HORIZON

Laughing Buddha sits down with Weeping
Sufi and they sing a song together

that sets fire to the furniture and makes the
river run backwards for a moment while its

fish inside change scales and close their
eyes for the first time in their lives

Hands move across a chessboard but no pieces move
Hair flies up in a breeze and comes down exactly where it
began each strand in place again and
ready for the next revelation

Their eyes lock in an embrace that shivers the coat rack of its
coats that fall in a disarrayed heap with all their
arms out straight as if in surrender or in
imitation of the cross

Laughing Buddha stops laughing for a
moment long enough for Weeping Sufi to
wipe his eyes and the

flock of geese overhead to check their
inner compasses and redirect their flight home

11/7

2 TWO SNORTING HORSES DASH DOWN A HILL

Laughing Buddha and Weeping Sufi agree it would be
unfair to write a series of poems in their
honor since no one could quite get at the
essence of either although as they'd be the

first to admit a flamingo might as it
sieves the water for food leaning its long
pink neck down and dipping its curved
beak into the murk back and forth endlessly back and forth
and Laughing Buddha agrees and Weeping Sufi disagrees
and vice versa until Weeping Sufi laughs a little and
Laughing Buddha grows grim then neutral then
goes far in to where no one can reach him
even the universe disappears

And Weeping Sufi stays seated on the cool riverbank and
floats down the green river in long watery
motions simultaneously and also
becomes the firefly-filled air making their
illuminated commas in it as it circulates past them into
an exponentially greater air

11/7

3 ONE WHOLE WHALLOP WON'T CURE THE ITCH

They are never alone and in their company no one is
ever alone yet none seem as alone as they

in such moments as the covering of an opening with one hand
or the pouring of tea carefully into a glass
or the sudden uncovering of an opening with one hand while

slowly covering an opening with the other

and they can see in each other's face each other's
face in return

11/8

4 A CRYSTAL PLUM HANGS FROM AN OPAL TREE

Laughing Buddha and Weeping Sufi sit looking at the sea

Laughing Buddha watches the heaving sea waves and
sometimes he counts them and sometimes he
doesn't

Weeping Sufi puts a shell to his ear and smiles then
sheds a tear for all the living and the dead and all those
yet unborn

The ocean stands up on its two hind legs for a second
and looks deeply into the oceans of their four eyes and says

"I am not lame and I am not forever
but only one can encompass me in both your
philosophies"

and sits down again then lies back as before
rippling its huge belly

Laughing Buddha turns to look at Weeping Sufi and
Weeping Sufi turns to look at Laughing Buddha

and just then millions of white sand crabs decide to
move as one a few yards to the left and sink
back down again into the sand

and the late morning sunlight through a late morning
haze spotlights their backs for a second
like twinkling stars before they disappear
leaving no trace they ever even existed
behind

11/8

5 BROKE AND DOWNHEARTED IN ¾ TIME

Laughing Buddha is the sadder of the two
Weeping Sufi the most joyous

A bouncing thing attracts their attention
then a silent thing then nothing at all

Weeping Sufi sees a ball of sunlight rise inside him
Laughing Buddha sees a black cloud float across

Nothing possible prevents them from the full apprehension of the
simplest presentation of anything facing them

Eager to arrive at the distant city many
travelers leave their burdens at the gate
where Laughing Buddha sits across from
Weeping Sufi chewing thoughtfully

I don't know if this will lead anywhere

But there's a small boat down there on the
vast open sea like a still opal surrounded on all sides by a
stunning white immensity

and Laughing Buddha and Weeping Sufi
each with the other's dispositions firmly in tow

are taking turns navigating under its
scarlet sail against a sharp golden sky

across black and endless waters

above a silvery light of the deepest depths invisible
except to intuitive lantern-fish and the

untroubled insights of the dead

11/8

6 SAND THROUGH A TINY HOLE YET THE HOURS DISAPPEAR

Laughing Buddha and Weeping Sufi
have a cat

Actually it's a lion

OK sometimes a cat sometimes a lion

And they don't actually "*have*" it the way you
have a cold or own a piece of furniture

It would be better to say "*they feed a
cat*"

The lion they feed themselves

By which I mean they feed *themselves* to the lion

Laughing Buddha looks his old regal self
riding the lion in the Assembly Hall of the Buddhas

Weeping Sufi is one of the Chosen Near Ones as well so he
often appears astride the lion
in peoples' dreams signifying a high state of attainment

The cat will curl up in their laps and they
have to stay in that position until it wakes up

They also curl up in a lap from time to time
the way a wind curls up inside a tempest
or a curve curls up inside a wave until it
breaks

The lap of a Self greater than themselves

An absence Who is a Greater Presence than any known

Feeding the cat is often a matter of
doing nothing since they also have many mice
in the same way they "*have*" a cat in that their fallen crumbs
feed the mice who live just behind the walls

Feeding the lion is another matter but it is done
periodically invisibly and often

When one of them isn't there he is
off "*feeding the lion*"
and by "*not there*" I mean he might be there visibly

The lion who roams freely from world to world
and whose roars between worlds alert its modest citizens both
human and otherwise to be on guard

and who is docile in between worlds and
fierce in either one once he's fully entered them

No self is exempt from this feeding in fact but
Laughing Buddha and Weeping Sufi offer themselves
voluntarily beforehand knowing that in so doing
they cause less trouble in the world and

less trouble in the world even by just the power of two is
actually a formidable improvement if only we

knew

11/9

7 BRIGHTNESS OVER YOUR SHOULDER AUGURS MOONLIGHT

A leaf falling will make Laughing Buddha laugh

A leaf falling will make Weeping Sufi weep uncontrollably

The appearance and disappearing of worlds makes
one laugh and the other weep

Now the laughter takes place way back in the brain of
Laughing Buddha and it is a laughter like the
songs of birds or the sound of the leaf itself as it
flitters through the air on its way down and the
sound it makes when it lands so softly as to be
almost unnoticed except for its tiny crinkle

The tears of the Sufi come from way down in the
heart of the Sufi the way sap rises to give
birth to a leaf on the tip of its branch and then one day
lets go of it and it falls so gracefully onto the
Autumn ground with all the other yellow leaves

And they are tears not of sorrow but they come
unexpectedly and often bringing with them a song like this one

the same way Laughing Buddha might have a phrase or two
after his bubbling laughter along the lines of
"One leaf has fallen
there's nothing left to do"

or *"The sound of one leaf falling…"*

and then he'll laugh and sit quietly

until dinnertime

11/9

8 TREES WEEP IN SILENCE IN THE NIGHT

Laughing Buddha and Weeping Sufi go rowing
and as they slide along the stream suddenly

Laughing Buddha asks the famous question:
"Is it the land moving or is it ourselves?"

Trees and rocks and tall grasses with an occasional
lion looking out with its face neutral but fierce as fire
or gaggles of geese gobbling by and maybe even a farmer in
straw hat or some giggling children

but from the point of view of the central core the
apex and visionary vantage pivot of contemplative
serene illumination

the burning question remains:
Is it the boat moving or the shore?

Are we going through life like blind astronomers
or is life moving around us like Saturnine movie projections from
a shepherd's bell or a cowherd's horn
and if so who's projecting it?

Weeping Sufi pulls harder on the oars
Laughing Buddha's laughter fills a glass jar with
Bluebottle flies and bright orange and black Monarch
butterflies in spirals

then suddenly from nowhere a star-like
apparition appears as apparitions must in the

air between them so that a kind of shimmering
mirror faces each from their prow or bow end of the skiff

and they see their slightly though not overly
astonished faces with their own living eyes there

looking very vivid and seeing what they see in them

and Weeping Sufi laughs just as a neutral lion roars
and Laughing Buddha sees fast geese flying overhead

and his face bursts with a happy goose-like look
that detached smile

as the little boat slides by
and the shore slides by

and the two revolve like moon and stars
sliding through the sliding sky

11/10

9   THE DOOR KNOCKS AND OPENS AND NO ONE'S THERE

There's always a secret to be found out

A kernel inside the shell to be searched

And while things are as they are and even
just are by being what they are
there's not only this nagging feeling but also an
entire dimension of meaningfulness however it may be
camouflaged in apparent straightforwardness or simple

laziness

that keeps Laughing Buddha and Weeping Sufi awake over all
as they ponder their holy texts and look up from them at
lightning bolt happenstance or bridges bursting into flame or flying
debris resembling the shadowy schemes of half-angels
of whom there are a secret number
though *"you shall know them by their acts"* certainly
resonates

Laughing Buddha sits way back and closes his eyes
Weeping Sufi sees figures moving among the charmed and smoky
forms like a ghostly perpetrator or a faulty
memory and calls out to it

And it emerges from head to foot the stalwart
demon of the piece which Weeping Sufi has to
subdue by means of whatever subtle or brute force he has

until the dawn of a new day slices him in two
and Weeping Sufi can also lean back with
eyes closed alit incandescently

Laughing Buddha opens his eyes and glances once at
Weeping Sufi and chuckles gently

11/11

10 WHILE STRAY BIRDS WHISTLE LOOSE LEAVES WHINNY

A shallow description of Laughing Buddha and
Weeping Sufi might include their
physical characteristics such as

facial hair or lack thereof and length of neck or
fingers how many arms and general height

So one is tall and short fat and thin while the
other is thin and fat short and tall for
example and both wear coarse cloth as well as
tailored suits and look both anonymous and

outrageously natural barefoot with patched robes
and bareheaded in sun or rain throats exposed

Though each one's face is both moonlike and sunlike and
each one's movements both smooth and
intensely minimal and clear

Both go from A to B with profound determination but as
light as feathers or falling leaves

Both throw themselves down in prostration as
naturally as breathing and maybe to the same
God a Being so difficult to ascertain by our mere
human apprehension whether yes or no

Though Laughing Buddha laughs happily at its
hints and suggestions as well as its
fully revealed apparitions in sunlight or moonlight as boldly as the
face of a flower

And Weeping Sufi sheds copious tears at
his own lacks as well as at
God's abundantly clear and precise Perfection
as for example in the workings of fate and
the antennae of gnats

Their eyes above all have no clouds in them no
overcast skies no impenetrable veils

Both their faces redefine nakedness of expression whether of
joy or expectation neutrality or repose as well as
consternation and pained wells of empathy so deep the
outmost planets shine back from their black waters' surfaces

As they curve their arms around and resume their
natural dispositions returning to complete Zero which
might be the same as the number One in its totality

bearded and clean shaven bald as light itself and
with hair to their shoulders in rivers of oiled ringlets

straight backed or prostrate

laughing or weeping

11/11

11 DREAMS COME TO THE WALNUT BUT NOT TO THE PEACH

The figures in their parables parade through the air like
ghosts shedding leaves like trees

assuming shape the way smoke drifts in the air after a
puff from somewhere
these metaphorical phantoms filled with the
momentary light of life from Laughing Buddha's

paradoxical sense of humor and Weeping Sufi's
sense of the poignant unpredictability of God in almost
all circumstances

Reversals of fortune in both directions and the utter
abandonment of hopelessness in all circumstances forming
the gist of their talks to each other and to
whomever else might circulate in their unwobbly orbits for a
time

Dramas unfold in Ozone Theater before
everyone's eyes and aswim in everyone's ears
and occasionally slip into the minds or hearts of the
listeners depending on the weather and whether their feet are
cold or hot and just how much
money might be in their pockets but for

Laughing Buddha and Weeping Sufi it is the
setting out of sweetmeats and the cordial exchange of
pleasantries to portray the deeper clangs and clamors of
mortal combat with hostile forces in this world and in themselves
and the dark impatient captain of death's boat always
about to set sail that animates their

parabolic conversations whether or not the moon hangs in a
green and cloudless sky or is wrapped in the
cloudy gauzes of storms and they have to take sudden shelter
with their eager listeners under a rock cliff or in a

hut somewhere or in a downtown coffee shop
at the corner of say Pine and Twelfth

11/16

12 SOPORIFICS TEND TO SLEEP LATE SAID PANDA DARLING

Dewdrops parachute slowly to the ground
a dray horse grins at its reflection in the snow
butterflies huddle together on a branch

as Laughing Buddha and Weeping Sufi watch
from their perspectives

each at the end of a perpetual cantilever
and each emphatically compassionate even when
asleep

though awake is the day side of their night being
sleep is the starry firmament with its long
lunar landscapes full of herons and other watchful predators who
stalk quietly at night by moon's light

until daylight opens their eyes again on the day's doings
from their always awake circumferences

Laughing Buddha and Weeping Sufi
consciousnesses balancing on the head of a pin
in corridors of light and blended voices

11/17

13 (ON WRITING A POEM)

You use everything you know and a lot of what you
don't know when you write a poem

It may be that you use more of what you don't know
than of what you know

It's best to make a run for it when you write a
poem rather than creep up to it hoping to
catch it unawares for then it might be so
asleep as to be unwakeable

The best poems don't come completely from us at all
nor from anyone else

If you call it dictation it's like wearing a very
tight-fitting sky-diving suit until suit is almost
indistinguishable from skin except that with just skin
we might crash to earth at too dangerous a
velocity

Go silent if the next line doesn't come and
wait like a cat at a mouse hole and
in a moment but only in a moment
it will tell you itself phrase by phrase

The first line should come as if in a dream
or an order barked at you from Elsewhere
and you can tell if there's more to come or not
from a soft knocking under the coffin lid
full of sunlight

Someone said and I agree
that in our normal walking-around waking state
we're idiots
but when actually composing poems
we're the greatest
geniuses in the world
and if this isn't one's
modus operandi then watch out for
arrogance delusion and ineptitude

Everyone approaches a poem their own way
but respect must be owed it the way you'd
respect an immigrant just arrived at Ellis Island
with little English and no sure destination

Poets that have only themselves as Source
must be saints or their poems may leave an
empty aftertaste

It's always good to wake up in the morning after a
good poem

11/17

14 THERE WAS NEVER A SANTA CLAUS BUT NEITHER WAS THERE NEVER NOT

When they leave their tea and wander through the
woods a kind of gauzy curtain falls behind them
and they're in another space than ours where

great discoverers stand on promontories looking through
spy-glasses and extraordinarily brilliant scientists isolate the
cancer cell successfully in a top floor laboratory that
changes the course of history entirely

Laughing Buddha is silent and Weeping Sufi dry-eyed
their two faces half-shadowed moon-phases
as they lean slightly together like two gentle drunks
and throw the 6-dimensional puzzle into the air and
watch it descend in slow spirals solving itself with
each turn and with each turn revealing another vast
panorama of nature like a mental
projection in full color and multifaceted
such as crashing waves against giant basalt rocks on a seashore or
African pampas grass blowing in one direction all day long
as if someone were incessantly
combing the tall and now-bending grasses golden

11/18

15 IF WE TELL YOU YOU WILL SEE THROUGH DARK WINDOWS

An elephant comes and sits down between them
to have its dinner

Never mind the tons of grass an adult elephant needs each
day to keep going we find this elegant pachyderm
with its ancient cracked epidermis

sitting happily though with that sublimely neutral
expression on its face and those two widely
separated beady eyes like those of whales

and indeed we could be at sea or deep in the
deep blue with this situation of giant

lumbering consciousness here between these two expert and
excellent human beings who don't miss a beat
but pass the elephant the plate of biscuits and eggs and pour him
a cup of hot tea with milk

And so the three of them sit in the fading sun
trunk sniffling around for tidbits and

Laughing Buddha and Weeping Sufi carrying on as
usual and very mindful of their guest though not
in the least perturbed or alarmed by his presence

If only we could feel this way when the huge bulk of
elephant might be the terrible sense of

emptiness without beauty without stars or night or
day with its lights and excuses

and though we throw dust onto our backs in
humble anonymity to cool off from our constant

mortal annoyance still we often ourselves sit between
laughter and weeping perhaps with our large
ear-flaps hanging and our eyes weary and watery

"Pass the tomatoes dear Sufi brother"

"And please pass the bread crusts my enlightened friend"

Then there's a loud trumpeting and a sudden
getting-to-its-feet of a few thousand pounds of
mammalian flesh and bone in a hurry to

join his herd as he snuffs an exhalation of
"thank yous" out his so excellently expressive proboscis

now diminishing in the distance to squint-sized
thumb dimensions among the trees

"Were you here a moment ago?" asks Laughing Buddha

*"Did you see the space that overbrimming
heartbeat occupied?"* says Weeping Sufi

11/19

16 THE TITLES ARE COMPOSED SEPARATELY FROM THE POEMS

But as one falls asleep the other wakens
or as one wakes up the other drowses

Though this isn't exactly true since neither are
asleep or awake but of another state over which
masks and gestures of sleeping and waking can be
slipped and they can slide into "*normal*" society unawares
either asleep or awake the way

zebras might stand in shoulder-high grass with their
black and white zigzags and virtually
disappear

One sings the other stays silent

One speaks the other opens an inner ear so
huge eight oceans with their incessantly
beating waves can fit easily into its shell

And yet few see them as anything but
creatures susceptible to waking and sleeping

speaking loudly or softly or keeping still
waving their hands or leaving them clasped
waterfall darkness catapult dove release southward
light so dazzling so incandescent they simply

smiling

11/22

17 HAVING SAID "GOOD MORNING" THE DAY FLICKERS AWAKE

At some point you have to get up
cross the world to get to the other
side before either chicken or egg drops to the pavement

Go through that Gate that gateless Gate

All that comes into focus and all that goes out again

Beyond but also within and preceding words any
unpacked dromedary might utter into its oats

And come back and take your seat again
at the selfsame pushbutton source of dawn and sunset
extravaganza productions
picture flash and picture sizzle
negative proof positive
positive proof negative

As her majesty the black cat Raven jumps to the
foot of the bed and starts purring in utter catlike
contentment all over again

11/24

18 GOOD GRAY TYGER IN THE MIRROR BURNING BRIGHT

~ On the birthday of William Blake

The mysticism of Laughing Buddha and the mysticism of
Weeping Sufi lands on them as lightly as a leaf

They wrap it around them like mossy blankets
against the cold

Speak its phrases both forwards and backwards and
draw its figures in the clean white sand at their
feet

Both smile at its greeting and frown at its
departure and often the
other way around

A diagram of earth and heaven may be
hovering above them as well as numerous
rustling sounds

They often open a door in nowhere and
walk right through

Their students see them go and eagerly
await their return which takes place almost as
casually

Laughing Buddha and Weeping Sufi
emerge back into themselves just in
time to lift a teacup to their lips with
laughing or weeping eyes

Even the stars twinkle differently around them

Gain and loss both seem insignificant in their domain

Every precious mote or moment is made the
most of

Time comes to a standstill in their presence

Laughing is weeping and weeping laughter
ringing down halls and corridors
while they remain perfectly still

The question of God never comes up because His
radiance is unmistakable to both
one naming Him one not

They stand up in a shower of snowflake stars

They sit down to the sun on one side and the
moon on the other

They themselves slowly revolve

And the planets follow

11/28

19 THE HO-HO SONG CAN ONLY GO ON SO LONG

One day Death comes in and sits down between
Laughing Buddha and Weeping Sufi
while they're having tea or maybe

walks between them while they're chatting or
squats between them while they're doing a little
gardening and casually mentioning the fact of
change or the richness of decay

And Death wears that quizzical expression and
looks at them with those very clear turquoise eyes we've
come to expect from Death

And Death makes it also very clear this is only a casual drop-in
not a rendezvous so they don't have to

gather any particular atmosphere around them or
prepare for the long journey or compose a
deathbed poem or put their
affairs in order to make their last repentances and pleas
or re-experience the deepest moments of their
living consciousness which once seemed like
taste of death to them now tested against the reality at last

This is only a social visit as it were

And Laughing
Buddha seems a little sorrowful and grim
to find death has undone so many
and faced with Death his usual silence becomes
the height of eloquence as all the small flowers by his
feet fade and turn brown

And Weeping Sufi wipes a tear away and asks Death
if they can bring anything for him or her as the
case may be saying how he's been looking forward to a
visit and seems to be gazing lovingly past Death's
face to some unseen space
beyond its variable form

And Death says no it has everything it needs

and is neither hungry nor satiated thirsty or
drunk but just sits between them it says
knowing they wouldn't be too put out or

astonished by such a visit as others might
getting up briefly to touch a butterfly whose day has
come to a close or breathe in some used-up air or
lay its hands gently on the surrounding woods long enough for
winter's hibernation to chill them into momentary sleep

Then sits down again between them and starts a long
soliloquy about its lengthy existence and dearth of true
friends after all this time cycle after cycle

eon after eon and makes mysterious mention of its
time before creation its endless moment of

stasis before the appearance of life itself which it
implies is not just brother or sister to itself

nor even its essence after all but the

exact same thing as itself seen from a

proper perspective

And Laughing Buddha's eyes wrinkle with laughter

And Weeping Sufi's eyes fill with glorious
tears to hear such words

And Death gets up and bows to both without
touching and leaves as effortlessly and anonymously as it

arrived and just as

unannounced

11/30

20 SEVERAL EXCELLENT RECIPES FOR SOUP ON A WINTER'S DAY

Laughing Buddha and Weeping Sufi attend to the
details of everything as if they were
galaxies coming to birth

noticing subtleties in a person's expression or the
way someone holds his or her shoulders or
hangs his or her head in just such a morning
light

Noticing things sometimes that haven't even seemed to
have happened yet though perhaps they
have

Flashing in full detail before eyes of theirs that
precede the eyes they use to see what's
actually in front of them

Laughing Buddha seeing the Light of Bodhi burst
out of the nut at the center of things

Weeping Sufi seeing one of the Divine Attributes perfectly
express itself with the clarity of a
hillside of white horses or the pouring of
liquid from a spout no faster than it
needs not to spill a drop in its gurgling transit

They rise as natural phenomena and sit again
as if they were herons after a long
migration folding their legs underneath them for
a rest

They walk with gentle determination knowing their
right and their left their front and their back
and who momentarily inhabits each section that is always
changing as if the central fixed point is on a
swivel rather than fixed in the ground like a
flagpole or a bomb about to explode

They tend to the details of everything like night nurses in a
hushed hospital checking charts

or like slowly outspiraling star debris from a
new galaxy coming to birth

12/1

21 DO YELLOW BUTTERFLIES GET THE BLUES?

Often when Laughing Buddha sits down his head tells him things
and when Weeping Sufi sits down his heart speaks to him

which if they ignore might cause harm
or at least lack of benefit

Things maybe not earthshaking or life-changing but which
kind of spell themselves out in sparkling neon or
perhaps come in the form of semi-audible whispers

but Laughing Buddha and Weeping Sufi know in their
heads and hearts and bones that they should act on them now or risk
floodwaters overflowing the city's sandbags or the
small plastic item in the machine catch fire and burn down the
house or the son of the rice farmer down the road
fail to secure the horse behind the rickety fence
no one else has noticed is about to fall apart
in the first wind

which Laughing Buddha sees for a photographic flash in his
mind while idly contemplating the rotten structure of exactly
that fence not some abstract symbolic fence
attended by angels

And Weeping Sufi might see a symbolic fence attended by
hosts of angels in his heart which swings open at a
touch to let the ailing mother through so that he knows if she
drinks enough pure water she'll completely recover

Just as in this poem that came to me at
seven in the morning but I was sleepy and wanted to
go back to sleep then realized it was like the
poem itself ironically and if I

ignored it I'd lose it but if I roused myself to
write it out as heard in heart and head and bones I'd at least
not cause possible lack of benefit and
it would be an actual example in itself of

what it's about

12/2

22 I SAW THE RED CARDINAL EATING AT OUR FEEDER

Everything moves along a track

A cat sniffs its way through life

A ladybug lands on a hibiscus leaf and chews
for a while then takes off

Rivers keep cutting their variously invariable way
through the same troughs season after season

Laughing Buddha becomes the light in the forest

Weeping Sufi disappears into the surrounding air

Their voices etch grooves that can be heard
like records by interested passersby on their
own way somewhere

Migrating geese in gorgeous high altitude flocks
pass along roughly the same routes generation after
generation goslings getting the etch-a-sketch somehow
into the seemingly arbitrary trajectories of their beings

Laughing Buddha puts down his tea glass with a
gentle crash

*"I'm not here now and I'll
never pass by here again!"*

A drip from rain on the roof drops onto
a rock and

Laughing Buddha laughs

12/2

23 PENCILS SHARPENED FOR ACTION PENS NIBBED IN THE BUD

Laughing Buddha and Weeping Sufi eat their sandwiches
then get back to the business of not eating their sandwiches

They get up and cross the room then get
back to the business of not getting up and
crossing the room

They deal with some prickly difficult situation
then get back to the business of not
dealing with some prickly difficult situation

as they watch out a window a hill of wild horses
gallop into seas of dust and back out again
then clouds gather and thunder-crash and
shrill lightning light up the room and seem to
lift it higher into the air than it would a
leaf or feather and spin it around

and Laughing Buddha turns to Weeping Sufi and
Weeping Sufi draws out his pen and writes a
treatise then gets back to the business of

not writing a treatise and Laughing Buddha is
nowhere to be seen getting back to the business of
sitting next to Weeping Sufi who gets back to the
business of not sitting next to Laughing Buddha

And the earth stops and starts so quickly in its course we
don't experience it as anything but smooth flow
and oceans pause then stop pausing and the
air itself stutters then stops stuttering

And all our traumas and icy-handed cruelties both
given and received stop in mid-flight or mid-
swing while tons of debris from both stars and
seafloor pour through
enough to create
another earth another galaxy

Then we resume again and could just as easily
walk off in another direction maybe even into
another dimension so that the

arc of trajectory fall somewhere in Southeast Asia
or the Arctic Circle or a very cozy restaurant in
Vienna

Where Laughing Sufi and Weeping Buddha sit
now reading their menus and wondering aloud
what some of the choice specialties are
and how they're prepared

Then get back to the business of lowering their eyes again
then raising them on the Serengeti Plains
or the plain fact of a room filled with

daylight

that gets back to the business of simply
being a room filled with daylight

12/4

24 I SHALL NOT AND WILL NOT CARRY A TUNE

At the first snowfall of winter Laughing Buddha and Weeping Sufi
see the world become more as they usually see it

seemingly substantial and insubstantial both
materially continuous and dazzling with a sparkling light

quiet and smooth-cornered with all its various jumble of
objects somehow glamorously ermined and
cuddled in homogeneity

Laughing Buddha's and Weeping Sufi's footprints through the
sparse woods not that dissimilar to the
prints of deer or raccoon even titmouse or field mouse
though on a smaller scale

And Laughing Buddha wonders about ants underground
in what must be frigid earthworks and chilly
tunnels and sees for a fantasy flash wisps of breath fog in
front of each one's mandibles and laughs

And Weeping Sufi puts seed out in a dish for the birds and the
dish fills with soft flakes that cover the seed with a
bright granular blanket

But like divine traces the seeds will be
revealed again as the light flakes melt
and the air thaws

And the unearthly quiet Laughing Buddha and
Weeping Sufi become themselves quiet in
gives way in light
at the end of snow season to
noise again

12/5

25 BRIGHT CANS OF BEANS ON FENCES FOR SHOOTING

There's a sensation to every cessation of sensation
and a cessation to every sensation

at which point Laughing Buddha and Weeping Sufi
at the actual borders of things and events
bow or turn in galactic directions as a light blue

wind blows around them

There's an eventual event of invincible eventuality
which is in itself an invincible event

at which point Laughing Buddha and Weeping Sufi
board a train leaving for Buffalo with bag lunches and
small books to read as the bright red landscape passes

There's an original origin to every orange
from which every orange originally originates

Laughing Buddha's face breaks out in a huge smile at this
that seems to take into its arc all the known and
unknown worlds and

Weeping Sufi takes the orange in his twelve hands and
peels it and gives some of the juicy sections to
Laughing Buddha some to a very old man to
his right and a very old woman in front of him and some
to several wisdom children of all colors to his
left and behind him and hundreds more sections to everyone circling the
circumference of the globe even unto the clouds

And there never seems to be an end to it that he
can tell as he continues peeling and
distributing original orange sections

with each blip of the beat and each new
original orange that comes into being

                                        12/6

26 I HEAR A POUNDING IN THE WALL AND IT'S NIGHTTIME

"Heaven may be at your fingertips" says Laughing Buddha
"*Oh would you please pass the jam*"

"Just as jam is at yours" says Weeping Sufi
"*Most gladly dear friend here's a biscuit*"

They're floating along in a sculpted golden cloud
just a few feet above the earth or well

maybe not really above the earth in a spatial way nor
at all in a condescending way but tops of

trees do seem to be passing by below them in a
kind of gliding manner and tops of buildings
stupas minarets and famous
bridges over wide waters

"Immanence and transcendence both" says Weeping Sufi
"simultaneously in the way that we might be

thinking of angels while frying an egg at the stove say"

"*This jam is bittersweet*" answers Laughing Buddha

"*This bread is brittle crumbly*"

And at that point the sun shows her face
and her golden fingers trace light delicately between the
teacups and plates and though they are not

alone in the usual sense there are of course the
requisite sprites djinn satvas and woodland creatures
or aerial denizens such as floating terns on gentle updrafts or
will-o-the-wisps which we don't often see circulating
around them listening to their labyrinthine dialog

At the same time both and each are in circulations of their
own which their words propel

"That Divine Presence both within and deeply connected"
says Weeping Sufi

"And above or without and completely disconnected"
says Laughing Buddha

Though no one sees them enter it exactly they agree that at
a certain point both Laughing Buddha and Weeping Sufi kind of
disappear altogether in the tea they sip and the

morning air

12/9

27 UPSWING AND DOWNSWING ARE THE SAME TO A GNAT

If it took place in the Amazon you'd expect

incredible fluted bright vermillion flowers and intricate
insects landing on them and sucking their nectar
and afternoon downpours that flood gullies and ditches and
pass on

And if it were the arctic things would get pretty hectic in the
white arithmetic of below zero conditions transpiring
in all directions except for the occasional
penguin and slow groan of glaciers and high-pitched whistling of
wheeling birds overhead

And if it were downtown Tokyo you'd expect trolley cars
clanging past and trolleys of tea things and general
traffic jams as well as toast and jam with tea

But it's none of these it's the highland and lowland it's
a warm and cool place out of the way where Laughing Buddha and
Weeping Sufi stand contemplating not the
passing scene exactly since in their eyes things

arise into existence in a constant interdependence
and fall away again or untangle in some very simple
way with the same suave ease with which they
tangled in the first place all in the
twinkling of an eye that acts as a
corridor interspace to one who knows Allah or
perhaps Nothingness might slip through into other
domains and disappear altogether from this one

And Laughing Buddha remembers his childhood kicking around
lavish palace grounds and sheds a tear for their oblivious ignorance

and Weeping Sufi sees where he is as opposed to
where he's been and laughs for a moment long and as
sweetly as water falling or a fountain of water rising in gushes
by natural push or pull out of pure gratitude

And all around their standing forms in the fading light
are dimensions and intercommunicating vesicles some
seen some unseen which some they
see and some they do not see

and if it were the Alps you'd expect to see
sheer blue shadows into steep nowheres from
blindingly white peaks blown in snow-mists and
avalanches and an air so thin and crisp it almost
shatters around you

and if it were the Black Forest a cuckoo clock might
cuckoo the hour and wake us from our

reverie

12/11

28 THE TOUCAN WITH ITS HUGE BILL PICKS BERRIES

Laughing Buddha wears a simple 100% cotton robe
with scoop collar distressed and worn with an
over-the-right-shoulder throw that can double as
light blanket by the side of the Ganges of faded saffron
with open toed and heeled sandals of non-animal fiber
by local craftsmen

Weeping Sufi wears a 100% wool hooded *djallaba*
floor-length in natural white or cream
large sewn patches in most areas though this season not
de rigueur that nevertheless provide highlight splashes of color
with skullcap of hand-knitted natural hemp
and matching sandals of goatskin handmade by himself

Or bits of scrap they may be rambling through
clinging to them as they pass bits of bird's nest or cobweb silk
sprig ends of cedar or pine

The shimmering mountain stream itself for evening wear as the
sun descends or the

night itself for nightwear as the

night arises all around them

the sound of sparrows in the morning as

early day's adornment

cloud light or cloudlessness

as the days progress

12/12

29 ONCE YOU SEE A CAT YOU PURR TOO

The broad lanes aren't broad enough for the
laughter of Laughing Buddha to resound and echo in

The high seas with their punctual whitecaps aren't
vast enough to contain Weeping Sufi's tears

And yet we carry on laughing and weeping from our
limited perspectives sometimes leading to excesses of
one or the other sometimes to a paucity of either

The winds blow south or north east or west with their
divine friendliness their eager velocities to carry our
tears or laughter into clouds of knowing and unknowing where
they might fall as rain or rays of light on fields such as

Van Gogh shot himself in the heart in or
explorers from one tribe or other first glimpsed golden
expanses under birds-egg blue skies and sobbed with
joy

Our hearts are halves for Laughing Buddha and
Weeping Sufi to bring together and make whole

Our raised voices can't contain enough silences for them to
hammer the halves together in and yet somehow they
do even in the general din

The dark cliff that faces us becomes an open thoroughfare

The entire sky bends down to brush our brow with
lips of brash acceptance

The first coin flung down on a red tile begins the
transaction in dream interpretation squares and circles
turning into their opposites night and day exchanging places
birds and lions somehow managing to metamorphose into
butterflies or battlements fluttering low over the
earth or actually embedded in it on entrenched stone foundations

I'll have sent the letter of my mortality and the reply will have
returned with forwarding address unknown as will we
all when all is said and done

But Laughing Buddha and Weeping Sufi have enough
ocean and enough sky to please them in
every circumstance

Yet never enough of either to continue their
feather-light cardiac expansion in which our

beats are encompassed in their deeper breaths
in the universe's endless contrapuntal cantilevers of

opposing rhythms of sky-lap ocean-swell earth-rotation
verbal squall balanced against the single beat of

silence that engulfs them all

12/14

30 A PUMPKIN ONCE STOOD UP AND SAT DOWN AGAIN IN A GOLDEN FIELD

"We've just met and yet I've grown old in
your presence," says Laughing Buddha one day a
few years after their first encounter

Weeping Sufi thinks of the great good fortune the
companion locus of divine unfoldings that
Laughing Buddha is to him and says

"If there is one bird and then two birds won't the
sky be crossed just that much faster?"

and weeps a little at the joy of that thought as they
turn in the road toward the abundant wheat fields
bending in near prostration then straightening up again as the
wind passes

Laughing Buddha's mother appears to him in a vision and then
just as instantaneously disappears but in that
noble moment stands against the sunlight and
warmth streams from her arms and face to him
in avalanche proportions

as he remains at his sublime axis and raises his
eyes again to meet Weeping Sufi's and sees

for a moment Weeping Sufi become a stalk of
living wheat a straight standing manifestation in creature form of
pure sunlight

12/16

31 SERENITY HAS MANY FACES AND ONE HEART

The roses Laughing Buddha and Weeping Sufi picked this
morning have come alive

They've opened their faces completely and their
petals have slowly spiraled out to reveal the
sensational scent of their deepest centers

into which and out of which all philosophy and
theology flow

Who sit together in human form as Laughing Buddha and
Weeping Sufi two figures out of the stuttering flowering of
time through the projector's slit so fast it seems
alive

though railroad trains may seem faster laser beams or the
speed of light itself yet

everything as the rose painstakingly shows us has its
time identical to itself the toad the turtle
the distracted rabbit the stone in the road they
saunter past and the

cantering colt frisky in morning sunlight who has
everything to look forward to and who
grows into a majestic mare in full gallop as

languorous petals fall

12/17

32 A LITTLE MANUAL OF STYLE

The direct experience of Laughing Buddha and Weeping Sufi is that

if rain falls they get wet and if it doesn't fall
they are dry through and through

in the sense that the Void who smiles so sweetly at
Laughing Buddha and surrounds each thing with its
own animate light as if little spectrums outlined each
caterpillar on each leaf and Laughing Buddha could
directly see that as well as the fluttering non-illusory illusion of its
butterfly flight not long down the road at the end of the leaf
into clear sky and so

laughs with its metamorphosis even past death though
grim at one turn is compassionately laughable at another

And for Weeping Sufi direct experience is that
no gap exits between the Name and the Named and the
original Holder of all Names the Light source and where the light
lands being God-drenched in a constant
light pulse always in motion as well as in
stillness but at each click a different set of
circumstantial universes at play all revealing the
pivotal singleness of purpose and compassionate action of God and
bringing tears to his eyes at the sight of it each
secondary and primary second each

chameleon turning color from nose-tip to tail as its
innermost surroundings dictate

No question for each of them what to do or
not to do what word to speak or withhold

No question at all to sit still or run like crazy to catch that
child falling from a high window into his arms

to sing or sit quietly to look in the mirror for a moment or
look away at the geese migration southwards or
northwards depending on the season thank you

and even thankful in true respect for the breathable
opportunity to do so

12/21

33 THINKING OF A NUMBER BETWEEN ONE AND ZERO

The road divided and split in two and the
two prongs of the fork went off in separate
directions and there were

lemonade stands on each road and behind the
rickety wooden table stood a glamorous temptress in white
and behind the other table at the other road stood a
well-behaved Boy Scout type with reddish cheeks and
kerchief tied around his neck although both have

fresh lemons cut and squeezed into perfect juice

"*Isn't that the way with roads*" laughs Laughing Buddha

"*In a few year's time there'll be a department store here and
we can nip in for a coat off the rack*" says Weeping Sufi

but I digress in fact I mightily digress because
at first I was going to have each of them go down one
road or other and up pop temptresses and Boy Scouts

while in fact it's one smooth single wide road
that meanders just enough to be comfortable

and though they're both on it they want to
cherish their time together so they

sit at the side of it and have a glass or two of
fresh squeezed lemonade from both Scout and
temptress who's a real vamp type with ringlet black
hair and slinky white silk gown but Laughing Buddha just
buys a glass and even looks into her moony face and
sees childhood and old age and death and
smiles

And Weeping Sufi buys a glass from the Boy Scout and
sees all that and the Resurrection and
pays him a little extra

12/24

TURN RIGHT AT THE STATUE WITH TWO HEADS

At some point we must recognize that
Laughing Buddha and Weeping Sufi are really
one person just as we are

and I don't mean this as a gimmicky metaphor
they're actually only one person but the

abiding characteristic is that he isn't here at all
not in a dead way and yet as absent as someone who's
died but whose soul is even more alive

A locus of consciousness an entity in which elegantly outrageous
things take place too amazing to enumerate as for example
the gossamer jets of each passing second or the

major cosmos expansion and contraction of each
ribcage lift and breath intake and release

though these may be somewhat superficial next to
rock ledge tilting his head thunderward in radiant
downpour or the averting of terrorist strike by an
eyeblink or the simple but profound thought of it
passing in his heart enough to deter disaster

and he combines in his Bodhisattvic compassion both
laughing and weeping as his face in the bus window reflects both
the distraught Puerto Rican mother eking out her living as well as the
craggy rock face of a mountain the straight highway's
cut through on its way to

glory

12/24

35 BUMPS IN THE ROAD EQUAL ROCKY TERRAIN AHEAD

The sky divers have finished sky diving
the nose divers have finished nose diving
the pearl divers have finished pearl diving
and have come up with no pearls

Laughing Buddha leans way over the edge and pats the
watery surface and his reflection crackles into eddies and then
ebbs placidly back into place again
as he cups a palm-full of water and drinks

Weeping Sufi is off in some cloud with his head definitely
massing together with other cumulus in order to
bring fresh rain to some parched fields on the
North Fork
though he's sitting next to Laughing Buddha gently dozing

"*We've been through so much already and there's
so much left to go*" he muses to himself in his sleep

(though he's not completely asleep)

"*Have I told you I love you yet?*" he hears back
from no one in particular and everyone

"*Have we heard all the arguments for losing every
vestige of hope?*" he hears answer

"*Then that settles it*" says Laughing Buddha who
wakes Weeping Sufi all the way up as he stands
above the pond and walks briskly away his
hands inside his wide sleeves

A family of gypsies is sauntering noisily by in their
vivid red and purple wagon pulled by an old horse up a dark hill

They sing "*Have I told you I love you yet?*" in
old Rumanian

A man running up the hill with a length of rope to
hang himself with yells "*I've lost all
vestiges of hope*" and flings one rope-end over a
low bough
and a flock of crows takes wing

Weeping Sufi stands up and spreads his arms
"*But there's one vestige of hope you haven't lost*" he shouts
"*and that's that I love you!*"

The man stops and falls in a heap

Laughing Buddha goes over and sits down next
to him and whispers the Secret Doctrine

The crows reassemble on that very low bough that
might have been the low-hanging bow of "enropetured" death

Weeping Sufi sees clouds part and a patch of
light light up a patch of darkness as the
gypsy wagon creaks out of sight to softly
repetitious accordion music

"*Have I told you I love you yet?*" in old Rumanian
fades into the dark trees

as the day settles around the crows and pulls in
its feathery black wings

1/1

36 CLANG CLANG CLANG GOES THE TROLLEY

From very high up in the air they can
as they say discern a light afar off

but it turns out to be Laughing Buddha and
Weeping Sufi

cutting the dark horizon like ships
heading home

They've compared every utterance and weighed and challenged every
thoughtless or thoughtful gesture and passing image both
cloudy and clear

They've said farewells to their respective mothers and
perspective has prevailed in which their
fathers like pirates have taken off their eye patches and
silenced their shoulder-parrots for just long enough to
be forgiven and to forgive in the

endless chain of generational misunderstandings and
unfilial anarchic resistance that seems to have to take
place for life on this planet to click forward a notch

So both Laughing Buddha and Weeping Sufi see the
light from a distance and are the light from a

distance though in both cases the distance isn't so
great it's more like they're right up here
next to us with each one's

wisdom somehow shedding its froth to the
clear depths inside the way morning mist burns off
while you're waiting for a pheasant to appear

"*What's that laughter I hear?*" one of them says

And the other says "*It's you!*"

"*And what's that weeping I hear then?*"
and the other or both say

"*It's the world's*"

1/2

37 BLACK CAT ON MY LAP WHIPPING HER TAIL

Death drops by again
but reassures Laughing Buddha and Weeping Sufi it's just
a social call

in the form of a fly with human face looking
winsomely up at them knowing it won't be
idly brushed away

Same fly that came to Blake and Dickinson though now a
little older though ageless and wiser though death is
only as wise as at the last moment the very
nanosecond before blackout or whiteout
what happens what thought action tipping the cabbie
paying back the debt incurring no new injustice
naming the Eternal One or sliding
transcendentally through like a lake of gliding swans

"*So how you boys doin'* " death might say
but doesn't it's as usual mute

"*Death is a bothersome fly today*" laughs
Laughing Buddha

"*Death my stepping stone my water bridge my starry lover my
passport out of here*" sighs Weeping Sufi

Death pauses and washes its hands and face before
proceeding then flies
straight for the cup-rim then the sugar cube

"*Death loves sweets*" says Laughing Buddha gravely
and sees a dying child in a blue nimbus

"*Its main nourishment*" says Weeping Sufi
"*though the bitter discontented unfulfilled and resistant
might go more noisily*"

Death stops and goes back the
way it came then turns and drops to a
lower decibel hovers then zooms away

as a leaf falls between them from the
highest tree

and a black sky reflects for a moment in their
steaming cups of tea

1/2

38   IT'S TIME FOR A BITE A SIP A LITTLE SLEEP

Laughing Buddha and Weeping Sufi sit listening to a
storyteller tell the story of Laughing Buddha and

Weeping Sufi and it isn't that different from
what they know to be the story of themselves

except that it's told in the third person and
in the past instead of in the eternal present

and sometimes it's Laughing Sufi and Weeping Buddha
and the rose held up in front of the attentive and
questioning congregation of thousands of Laughing Buddha's
disciples is a yellow tulip or a pine cone or a rusty thimble

though the rose in which Weeping Sufi unwraps his
soul petal by petal to core nakedness before The Absolute is not a
charging horse or a

roaring lion as so often happens in these stories or a falling
building or a forest fire but a real rose
of stunningly delicate hue and a central curling red flame

But the storyteller is talking directly to them and they are
listening as various flakes fall on them which are the

various flakes of passing time so that pretty soon
as time present continues forward in actual time the

storyteller slowly comes round to telling their story in the
present tense and Laughing Buddha and Weeping Sufi begin

meticulously receding into the recent then less recent
past the more the
storyteller tells their tale

So that even the rocks they're sitting on begin to look old

And the sparkle in the air shimmering everywhere

And the deeply listening trees

1/5

39 TAKE THREE AND CALL ME IN THE MORNING

Laughing Buddha and Weeping Sufi decide to take a
journey although people like them don't exactly
decide to take one action or another but seem to
receive subtle orders that instantly magnify into

perfect choices at any given moment something beyond our
narrow comprehension they go right or left down
this street or that as if drawn by a solar
magnet or gently propelled by a wind

and find themselves as they do now the two
friends at the doorway of someone unspeakably

suffering or about to make a very bad
decision which Laughing Buddha sees right away and
with one hand raised and the other lowered

neutralizes with a word and a slight smile
and the old woman bursts into tears to have been
stopped from a possibly fatal mistake

and now they stand on a bridge down the
road from that dwelling and large
trees are floating downriver underneath them in the
flashing foam and they know there's been a

hurricane upriver so they turn toward it and head
up a different road than the one they had

earlier intended

1/7

40 SO MUCH FOR FAREWELLS SAY THE ROOSTERS TO THE NIGHTTIME

Traveling light and depending on the bottomless
generosity of Reality the clothes on their backs and the
bare fact of being alive whose breaths include
pink blossoms in flower on lowering branches and
sheep in meadows munching the blades of their continual breakfasts
with sunlight on curly fleeces and
muzzles moistened by early morning dew glisten

Laughing Buddha and Weeping Sufi walk briskly into the
glowering darkness ahead with fierce determination and their
hands relaxed at their sides in easy motions
on their way to the source of the problem whatever it might
be in whatever interstice of time and space is

manifested at that congeneity of moments the intricate
meshing of theirs and its *modus operandi* though

theirs is aligned (as *its* is too actually) to a borderless sea and
horizonless sky stretched from earth to earth in which each

creature is an earthily celestial cosmos
reaching out of itself and calling out

the One True Name

through all things' variable complicities

1/7

41 IS IT TOO LATE TO CALL HOME?

The road winds around a strange mountain

strange forces both animal and human float forward then
retreat in the bluish mist enveloping the trees

Huts appear some with roofs and smoking chimneys
some roofless maybe walless doorless floorless even hutless

Laughing Buddha chants under his breath and
swivels in the mist disappear

Weeping Sufi recites under his breath and a way
opens up in a tall rock that is perhaps

a heart either his own or another's encountered along the
way as they walk through a sparse wood of

birch trees and slender oaks bent at the top to
let pale sunlight enter

and the two walk in silence the

rest of the way

42 A QUESTION WITH PROFOUND THEOLOGICAL IMPLICATIONS

If I saw me from outside me
would I like me?

43 NO ANSWER IS NOT AN ANSWER NOR IS SILENCE AN ASSERTION

Each of us recognizes our mortality separately

44 A BLUE SUNSET SITS ON AN ORANGE HORIZON

They trail their hands in the water

Their feet hit the cold hard ground

Their faces light up dark corners

Their eyes are wet with light

They move with a deep resilience

They fall into shadows and out again

People who meet them are amazed

They do nothing to attract attention

Their mode is invisibility

I've seen one or two of them close up

As in all of us most of them is hidden

As in all of us they dwell in sweetness

When a light in the dark is ignited

A spinning takes place like earth's orbit

1/10/2004

ABOUT THE AUTHOR

BORN IN 1940 in Oakland, California, Daniel Abdal-Hayy Moore's first book of poems, *Dawn Visions*, was published by Lawrence Ferlinghetti of City Lights Books, San Francisco, in 1964, and the second in 1972, *Burnt Heart / An Ode to the War Dead*. He created and directed The Floating Lotus Magic Opera Company in Berkeley, California in the late 60s, and presented two major productions, *The Walls Are Running Blood*, and *Bliss Apocalypse*. He became a Sufi Muslim in 1970, performed the Hajj in 1972, and lived and traveled throughout Morocco, Spain, Algeria and Nigeria, landing in California and publishing *The Desert is the Only Way Out*, and *Chronicles of Akhira* in the early 80s (Zilzal Press). Living in Philadelphia since 1990, in 1996 he published *The Ramadan Sonnets* (Jusoor/City Lights), and in 2002, *The Blind Beekeeper* (Jusoor/Syracuse University Press). He has been the major editor for a number of works, including *The Burdah* of Shaykh Busiri, translated by Shaykh Hamza Yusuf, and the poetry of Palestinian poet, Mahmoud Darwish, translated by Munir Akash. He is also widely published on the worldwide web: *The American Muslim, DeenPort*, and his own website, among others: www.daniel-moorepoetry.com

POETIC WORKS BY DANIEL ABDAL-HAYY MOORE

Published and Unpublished

(many to appear in the ECSTATIC EXCHANGE SERIES)

Dawn Visions (published by City Lights, 1964)
Burnt Heart/Ode to the War Dead (published by City Lights, 1972)
This Body of Black Light Gone Through the Diamond (printed by Fred Stone, Cambridge, Mass, 1965)
On The Streets at Night Alone – 1965 (?)
All Hail the Surgical Lamp – 1967
States of Amazement – 1970

The Chronicles of Akhira (1981) (published by Zilzal Press with Typoglyphs by Karl Kempton, 1986)
Mouloud (1984) (A Zilzal Press chapbook, 1995)
Man is the Crown of Creation (1984)
The Look of the Lion (The Parabolas of Sight) (1984)
The Desert is the Only Way Out (completed 4/21/84) (Zilzal Press chapbook, 1985)
Atomic Dance (1984) (am here books, 1988)
Outlandish Tales (1984)
Awake as Never Before (12/26/84) (Zilzal Press chapbook, 1993)
Glorious Intervals (1/1/85) (Zilzal Press chapbook, ?)
Long Days on Earth/Book I (1/28/85 – 8/30/85)
Long Days on Earth/Book II (Hayy Ibn Yaqzan) (1985)
Long Days on Earth/Book III (1/22/86)
Long Days on Earth/Book IV (1986)
The Ramadan Sonnets (Long Days on Earth/Book V) (5/9 –6/11/86) (Published by Jusoor/City Lights Books, 1996)
Long Days on Earth/Book VI (6-8/30/86)
Holograms (9/4/86 – 3/26/87)
History of the World (The Epic of Man's Survival) (4/7 – 6/18/87)
Exploratory Odes (6/25 – 10/18/87)
The Man at the End of the World (11/11 – 12/10/87)
The Perfect Orchestra (3/30 – 7/25/88)
Fed from Underground Springs (7/30 – 11/23/88)
Ideas of the Heart (11/27/88 – 5/5/89)

New Poems (scattered poems, out of series, from 3/24 – 8/9/89)

Facing Mecca (5/16 – 11/11/89)

A Maddening Disregard for the Passage of Time (11/17/89 – 5/20/90)

The Heart Falls in Love with Visions of Perfection (6/15/90 – 6/2/91)

Like When You Wave at a Train and the Train Hoots Back at You (Farid's Book) (6/11 –
    7/26/91)

Orpheus Meets Morpheus (8/1/91 – 3/14/92)

The Puzzle (3/21/92 – 8/17/93)

The Greater Vehicle (10/17/93 – 4/30/94)

A Hundred Little 3-D Pictures (5/14/94 – 9/11/95)

The Angel Broadcast (9/29 – 12/17/95)

Mecca/Medina Time-Warp (12/19/95 – 1/6/96) (Published as a Zilzal Press chapbook, 1996)

Miracle Songs for the Millennium (1/20 – 10/16/96)

The Blind Beekeeper (11/15/96 – 5/30/97) (Published 2002 by Jusoor/Syracuse University Press)

Chants for the Beauty Feast (6/3 – 10/28/97)

Open Doors (10/29/97 – 5/23/98)

Salt Prayers (5/29 – 10/24/98)

Some (10/25/98 – 4/25/99)

Flight to Egypt (5/1 – 5/16/99)

I Imagine a Lion (5/21 – 11/15/99)

Millennial Prognostications (11/25/99 – 2/2/2000)

The Book of Infinite Beauty (2/4 – 10/8/2000)

Blood Songs (10/9/2000 – 4/3/2001)

The Music Space (4/10 – 9/16/2001)

Where Death Goes (9/20/2001 – 5/1/2002)

The Flame of Transformation Turns to Light (99 Ghazals Written in English) (5/2 – 6/29/2002)

Through Rose-Colored Glasses (7/22/2002 – 1/15/2003)

Psalms for the Broken-Hearted (1/22 – 5/25/2003)

Hoopoe's Argument (5/27 – 9/18/03)

Love is a Letter Burning in a High Wind (9/21 – 11/6/2003)

Laughing Buddha/Weeping Sufi (11/7/2003 – 1/10/2004) (published 2005 by The Ecstatic
    Exchange)

Mars and Beyond (1/20 – 3/29/2004) (published 2005 by The Ecstatic Exchange)

Underwater Galaxies (4/5 – 7/21/2004)

Cooked Oranges (7/23/2004 – 1/24/2005

Holiday from the Perfect Crime (1/25 – 6/11/2005)

Stories Too Fiery to Sing Too Watery to Whisper (6/13/2005 –)